Cool SOUPS & STEWS

Easy & Fun Comfort Food

ALEX KUSKOWSKI

Checkerboard
Library

An Imprint of Abdo Publishing
www.abdopublishing.com

www.abdopublishing.com

Published by Abdo Publishing, a division of ABDO, PO Box 398166, Minneapolis, Minnesota 55439. Copyright © 2015 by Abdo Consulting Group, Inc. International copyrights reserved in all countries. No part of this book may be reproduced in any form without written permission from the publisher. Checkerboard Library™ is a trademark and logo of Abdo Publishing.

Printed in the United States of America, North Mankato, Minnesota
102014
012015

Editor: Liz Salzmann
Content Developer: Nancy Tuminelly
Cover and Interior Design and Production: Colleen Dolphin, Mighty Media, Inc.
Food Production: Frankie Tuminelly
Photo Credits: Colleen Dolphin, Shutterstock

The following manufacturers/names appearing in this book are trademarks: Allens®, Lea & Perrins®, Oster®, Osterizer®, Pyrex®, Quaker®

Library of Congress Cataloging-in-Publication Data
Kuskowski, Alex.
  Cool soups & stews : easy & fun comfort food / Alex Kuskowski.
    pages cm. -- (Cool home cooking)
  Audience: Age 7-14.
  Includes index.
  ISBN 978-1-62403-504-3
  1. Soups--Juvenile literature. 2. Stews--Juvenile literature.
  I. Title. II. Title: Cool soups and stews.
  TX757.K87 2015
  641.81'3--dc23
                    2014024637

SAFETY FIRST!

Some recipes call for activities or ingredients that require caution. If you see these symbols, ask an adult for help.

HOT STUFF!

This recipe requires the use of a stove or oven. Always use pot holders when handling hot objects.

SUPER SHARP!

This recipe includes the use of a sharp utensil such as a knife or grater.

NUT ALERT!

Some people can get very sick if they eat nuts. If you cook something with nuts, let people know!

CONTENTS

SERVING UP SOUP!

Fill up your family and friends at home! Homemade soups and stews are easy and **delicious**. You can serve them up hot or cold. Soup is great for dinner, lunch, or even breakfast!

Cooking food at home is healthy and tasty. It can be a lot of fun too. Many canned or frozen foods include unhealthy ingredients. When you make the food, you know exactly what's in it. It's easy to make a dish that's **unique** to you. Cook a recipe just the way you like it. Add fresh ingredients to make flavors pop. You can even share what you make with others.

Put the flavor back in your food. Start making home cooked meals! Learn how to serve up some delicious soup for your next meal. Check out the recipes in this book.

THE BASICS

Get your cooking started off right with these basic tips!

ASK PERMISSION

Before you cook, ask **permission** to use the kitchen, cooking tools, and ingredients. If you'd like to do something yourself, say so! Just remember to be safe. If you would like help, ask for it! Always get help when you are using a stove or oven.

BE PREPARED

Be organized. Knowing where everything is makes cooking safer and more fun!

Read the directions all the way through before you start. Remember to follow the directions in order.

The most important ingredient of great cooking is preparation! Make sure you have all the ingredients you'll need.

Put each ingredient in a separate bowl before starting.

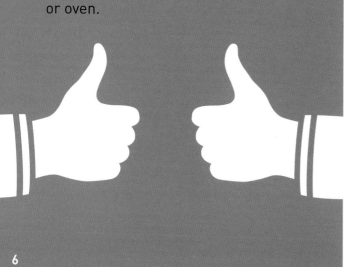

BE SMART, BE SAFE

Never work at home alone in the kitchen.

Always have an adult nearby for hot jobs, like using the oven or the stove.

Have an adult around when using a sharp tool, such as a knife or grater. Always be careful when using them!

Remember to turn pot handles toward the back of the stove. That way you avoid accidentally knocking them over.

BE NEAT, BE CLEAN

Start with clean hands, clean tools, and a clean work surface.

Tie back long hair so it stays out of the food.

Wear comfortable clothing and roll up long sleeves.

COOL COOKING TERMS

HERE ARE SOME HELPFUL
TERMS YOU NEED TO KNOW!

CUBE

Cube means to cut something into small squares.

BOIL

Boil means to heat liquid until it begins to bubble.

DICE

Dice means to cut something into very small squares.

CHOP

Chop means to cut into small pieces.

DRAIN

Drain means to remove liquid using a strainer or **colander**.

MINCE

Mince means to cut or chop into tiny pieces.

SHRED

Shred means to tear or cut into small pieces using a grater.

PEEL

Peel means to remove the skin, often with a peeler.

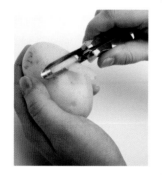

SIMMER

Simmer means to cook something so it bubbles gently.

PUREE

Puree means to mix something in a blender until it is liquid.

SLICE

Slice means to cut food into pieces of the same thickness.

COOL TOOLS

HERE ARE SOME OF THE TOOLS YOU WILL NEED!

blender

cutting board

large pot

measuring cups (dry)

measuring cup (wet)

measuring spoons

medium saucepan

mixing bowls

mixing spoon

peeler

plastic zipper bag

pot holders

serving bowl

sharp knife

spoon

strainer

whisk

COOL INGREDIENTS

HERE ARE SOME OF THE INGREDIENTS YOU WILL NEED!

avocado

basil	bay leaves	beef stew meat	black beans
blueberries	carrots	celery	cilantro
cornstarch	crushed tomatoes	cucumbers	egg noodles

garlic

green beans

green onions

jalapeño pepper

kidney beans

olive oil

onion

potatoes

spinach

tomatoes

tomato paste

vegetable oil

white beans

white hominy

worcestershire sauce

zucchini

VEGGIE CHICKEN NOODLE

Serve up a new family favorite!

INGREDIENTS

1 tablespoon butter

2 cloves garlic, diced

½ cup chopped onion

½ cup chopped celery

1 cup sliced carrots

4 14.5-ounce cans chicken broth

1 14.5-ounce can vegetable broth

½ pound chicken breast, cooked and chopped

½ teaspoon dried basil

½ teaspoon dried oregano

2 bay leaves

2½ cups egg noodles

½ teaspoon salt

½ teaspoon pepper

TOOLS

measuring cups

measuring spoons

sharp knife

cutting board

2 large pots

mixing spoon

strainer

pot holders

1 Melt the butter in a large pot over medium heat. Add the garlic, onion, celery, and carrots. Cook and stir the mixture for 5 minutes.

2 Put the chicken broth and vegetable broth in the pot. Stir in the chicken, basil, oregano, and bay leaves.

3 Turn the heat to high. Bring the mixture to a boil.

4 Turn the heat down to medium. Cover the pot. Let the mixture simmer for 20 minutes.

5 Fill another pot with 5 cups of water. Bring the water to a boil over medium-high heat. Add the noodles. Boil them for 10 minutes.

6 Drain the water from the noodles. Add the noodles to the large pot. Simmer the soup for 5 more minutes. Stir in salt and pepper.

CREAMY TOMATO BASIL

Warm up with this savory soup!

1. Put the tomatoes, juice, and garlic in a large pot. Bring the mixture to a boil over high heat. Turn the heat down to medium. Let the mixture simmer for 30 minutes.

2. Put the mixture in the blender. Add the basil. Puree until smooth.

3. Put the mixture back in the pot.

4. Cook the mixture over medium heat. Add the cream, butter, salt, and pepper. Heat and stir until the butter melts.

MAKES 4 SERVINGS

INGREDIENTS

5 large tomatoes, chopped

4 cups tomato juice

2 cloves garlic, diced

½ cup basil

1 cup heavy whipping cream

½ cup butter, chopped

¼ teaspoon salt

¼ teaspoon pepper

TOOLS

sharp knife

cutting board

measuring cups

measuring spoons

mixing spoon

large pot

blender

pot holders

CHICKEN TORTILLA SOUP

Dig into this Tex-Mex soup!

 MAKES 8 SERVINGS

INGREDIENTS

2 tablespoons vegetable oil

2 chicken breasts, diced

2 cloves garlic, diced

1 jalapeño chili, diced

½ cup diced onion

5½ cups chicken broth

2 14.5-ounce cans crushed tomatoes

1 teaspoon chili powder

1 teaspoon cumin

1 teaspoon oregano

½ teaspoon salt

1 teaspoon garlic powder

1½ cup white hominy

1 14.5-ounce can black beans

1 teaspoon lime juice

1 cup cilantro

¼ cup sliced green onions

1 cup shredded pepper Jack cheese

1 avocado, peeled and cubed

½ cup crushed tortilla chips

TOOLS

sharp knife

cutting board

measuring cups

measuring spoons

large pot

mixing spoon

serving bowls

pot holders

1. Heat the oil in a large pot over high heat. Add the chicken, garlic, jalapeño, and onion. Stir and cook the mixture for about 10 minutes.

2. Stir in the chicken broth, tomatoes, and 1½ cups water. Add the chili powder, cumin, oregano, salt, and garlic powder. Stir well. Bring the mixture to a boil over high heat. Turn the heat down to medium-high. Simmer for 50 minutes, stirring occasionally.

3. Add the hominy, beans, lime juice, and cilantro to the pot. Simmer for 10 minutes, stirring occasionally.

4. Serve hot in bowls. Sprinkle green onions, cheese, avocado, and tortilla chips on top.

GARDEN VEGGIE STEW

Dig in to a chunky veggie stew!

 MAKES 6 SERVINGS

INGREDIENTS

2 teaspoons olive oil

1 cup chopped onion

2 teaspoons chopped oregano

4 garlic cloves, minced

6 cups chopped zucchini

3 cups chopped green beans

1 cup chopped carrots

1 cup corn kernels

4 cups chopped tomato, divided

3 cans chicken broth

2 tablespoons tomato paste

1 cup uncooked pasta

1 can white beans

1 can kidney beans

¾ cup spinach

¾ teaspoon salt

½ teaspoon black pepper

1 cup grated Asiago cheese (optional)

TOOLS

measuring cups

measuring spoons

sharp knife

cutting board

mixing spoon

large pot

blender

serving bowls

1 Heat the oil in a pot over medium-high heat. Add the onion. Stir and cook the onion for 3 minutes. Stir in the oregano and garlic. Cook for 1 more minute.

2 Add the zucchini, green beans, carrots, and corn to the pot. Cook the mixture for 10 minutes or until the vegetables become tender. Turn off the heat.

3 Put the tomato, 1¾ cup broth, and tomato paste in the blender. Puree the mixture until smooth. Add the mixture to the pot.

4 Turn the heat to medium-high. Bring the mixture to a boil. Add the pasta, beans, and remaining broth to the pot. Turn the heat to medium-low. Simmer for 20 minutes, stirring occasionally. Turn off the heat.

5 Stir in the spinach, salt, and pepper.

6 Serve the stew in bowls. Top with the grated cheese.

SAVORY POTATO & HAM SOUP

Try this mouthwatering meal!

MAKES 8 SERVINGS

INGREDIENTS

4 potatoes, diced
½ cup diced celery
⅓ cup chopped onion
½ cup chopped carrots
¾ cup chopped cooked
    ham
1 teaspoon black pepper
3⅓ cups chicken broth
5 tablespoons butter
5 tablespoons flour
2 cups milk

TOOLS

measuring spoons
measuring cups
sharp knife
cutting board
large pot
mixing spoon
medium saucepan
whisk

1 Put the potatoes, celery, onion, carrots, ham, pepper, and broth in a large pot. Bring the mixture to a boil over high heat.

2 Turn the heat down to medium. Cook and stir the mixture for 15 minutes.

3 Melt the butter in a saucepan over medium-low heat. Add the flour. Whisk for 1 minute.

4 Add the milk slowly, while stirring. Cook and stir for 5 minutes.

5 Add the butter and milk mixture to the large pot. Cook and stir for 5 minutes, or until the soup thickens.

BASIC BEEF STEW

Make a crowd pleaser with this hearty stew!

 MAKES 4 SERVINGS

INGREDIENTS

¼ cup flour

1 teaspoon garlic powder

1 teaspoon onion powder

½ teaspoon black pepper

2 pounds beef stew meat, chopped

3 tablespoons vegetable oil

2 cans beef broth

1 teaspoon rosemary

1 teaspoon parsley

3 large potatoes, cubed

4 carrots, diced

4 stalks celery, diced

1 onion, chopped

6 teaspoons cornstarch

1 tablespoon Worcestershire sauce

1 tablespoon ketchup

TOOLS

measuring spoons

measuring cups

sharp knife

cutting board

plastic zipper bag

large pot

mixing spoon

small mixing bowl

1. Put the flour, garlic powder, onion powder, and pepper in the plastic bag. Shake to mix the ingredients. Add the beef to the bag. Shake to cover the meat in the flour mixture.

2. Put the meat and vegetable oil in a large pot. Heat over medium heat for 10 minutes, stirring occasionally.

3. Add the beef broth, rosemary, and parsley. Stir. Bring the mixture to a boil over high heat.

4. Turn the heat down to medium-low. Cover the pot. Let the stew simmer for 1 hour.

5. Stir in the potatoes, carrots, celery, and onion. Mix the cornstarch and 6 teaspoons cold water together in a small bowl. Add the cornstarch mixture to the stew. Cover the pot. Simmer for 1 hour, stirring occasionally.

6. Stir in the Worcestershire sauce and ketchup.

CHILLED CUCUMBER SOUP

Cool down with a summer soup!

INGREDIENTS

2 cucumbers
2 tablespoons olive oil
4 green onions, sliced
2 cloves garlic, chopped
2 cups chicken broth
½ teaspoon salt
1 avocado, diced
⅛ tablespoon dill
3 tablespoons parsley
½ cup yogurt

TOOLS

measuring cups
measuring spoons
cutting board
sharp knife
peeler
spoon
large pot
blender
mixing bowl
mixing spoon

1. Peel the cucumbers. Cut them in half lengthwise. Use a spoon to remove the seeds. Chop the cucumbers into small pieces.

2. Heat the olive oil in a large pot over medium heat. Add the green onions and garlic. Cook for 5 minutes.

3. Add the cucumbers, broth, and salt to the pot. Turn the heat to medium-high. Cook the mixture for 8 minutes, stirring occasionally. Turn off the heat. Let the mixture cool.

4. Put the mixture in the blender. Add the avocado, dill, and parsley. Puree the mixture until smooth. Pour the mixture into a mixing bowl.

5. Add the yogurt to the mixing bowl and stir. Put the soup in the refrigerator for 1 hour. Serve cold.

VERY BERRY DESSERT

Sip up a sweet soup!

1. Wash the fruit in cold water. Cut off the tops of the strawberries. Chop them into small pieces.

2. Put the strawberries, blueberries, heavy cream, sour cream, milk, and vanilla in the blender. Blend on low until the mixture is smooth. Pour it into a mixing bowl.

3. Stir in the sugar and cinnamon.

4. Chill the soup in the refrigerator for 8 hours. Serve cold.

INGREDIENTS

3½ cups strawberries

1 cup blueberries

1 cup heavy cream

½ cup sour cream

1½ cups whole milk

1 teaspoon vanilla extract

½ cup white sugar

½ teaspoon ground cinnamon

TOOLS

measuring cups

measuring spoons

sharp knife

cutting board

blender

mixing bowl

mixing spoon

CONCLUSION

This book has some seriously **delicious** soup recipes! But don't stop there. Get creative. Add your favorite ingredients to the recipes. Cook it your way.

Check out other types of home cooking. Make tasty breads, main dishes, **salads**, drinks, and even **desserts**. Put together a meal everyone will cheer for.

WEBSITES

To learn more about Cool Home Cooking, visit booklinks.abdopublishing.com. These links are routinely monitored and updated to provide the most current information available.

GLOSSARY

colander – a bowl with small holes in it used to drain food.

delicious – very pleasing to taste or smell.

dessert – a sweet food, such as fruit, ice cream, or pastry, served after a meal.

permission – when a person in charge says it's okay to do something.

salad – a mixture of raw vegetables usually served with a dressing.

unique – different, unusual, or special.

INDEX